BOOK-LOVERS, BIBLIOMANIACS AND BOOK CLUBS

BOOK-LOVERS, BIBLIOMANIACS
AND
BOOK CLUBS

HENRY HOWARD HARPER

ISBN: 978-93-5420-803-4

Published: -

LECTOR HOUSE LLP
E-MAIL: lectorpublishing@gmail.com

L.Meynell

BOOK-LOVERS BIBLIOMANIACS AND BOOK CLUBS

BY

HENRY H. HARPER

PREFATORY

Having been asked to make a few remarks upon Book-loving, Book-buying, and Book Clubs,—not for publication before the great audience of readers, but for the exclusive use of the members of a private Book Club,—I venture thus to offer my views, hoping that in the light of my own personal experience I may be able to give a few useful hints and suggestions to those who may peruse the pages which follow.

If this little tome, in which are recorded the reflections of one who for many years has mingled with publishers, booksellers, bibliophiles, collectors, and bibliomaniacs, should prove to be of any interest or service, and is found worthy of a small space in some sequestered nook in the library, where it may in silent repose behold its more worthy and resplendent companions, the fondest ambition of the author will be gratified beyond peradventure.

The Author.

BOOKLOVERS, BIBLIOMANIACS AND BOOK CLUBS

Book-collecting is undeniably one of the most engaging pursuits in which a refined and artistic taste may be indulged. From the earliest times, and even before the days of printing, this pleasant diversion has been pursued by persons of moderate means as well as by those of wealth and distinction, and every succeeding generation of book-collectors has exceeded its predecessors in numbers and in enthusiasm. The alluring influences of bibliophilism, or book-loving, have silently crept into thousands of homes, whether beautiful or humble; for the library is properly regarded as one of the most important features of home as well as mental equipment.

In *The House Beautiful* William C. Gannett emphasizes the importance of considering the library as foremost in furnishing a home. He says: "It means admission to the new marvels of science, if one chooses admission. It means an introduction to the noblest company that all the generations have produced, if we claim the introduction. Remembering this, how can one help wishing to furnish his house with some such furniture? A poet for a table piece! A philosopher upon the shelf! Browning or Emerson for a fireside friend!

"A family's rank in thought and taste can well be gauged by the books and papers that lie upon the shelf or table of the library."

Not many years ago, Mr. Howard Pyle said: "I sometimes think that we are upon the edge of some new era in which the art of beautifying books with pictures shall suddenly be uplifted into a higher and a different plane of excellence; when ornate printed colour and perfect reproduction shall truly depict the labour of the patient draughtsman who strives so earnestly to beautify the world in which he lives, and to lend a grace to the living therein." The prophecy is already fulfilled, and a modern book, in order to win favor among present-day bibliophiles, must embody an harmonious assimilation of many arts.

The ardor of possessing books, commonly called bibliomania, also styled bibliophilism and "biblio"—whatever else that has suggested itself to the fruitful imaginations of dozens of felicitous writers upon the subject,—is described by Dibdin as a "disease which grows with our growth, and strengthens with our strength." Kings and queens have not been immune from this prevalent though harmless malady. The vast resources of Henry VII were employed in collecting a library of which a modern millionaire collector might be justly proud. Many specimens of his magnificent collection, bearing the royal stamp, are now to be found in the British Museum. Queen Elizabeth and Lady Jane Grey were submissive victims of the bibliomania. It is worthy of note that while there were but few women book-collectors in the Elizabethan period, there are at the present time in our own country almost as many women as there are men engaged in this fascinating pursuit. As late as 1843, Dibdin remarks that "it is a remarkable circumstance, that the bibliomania has almost uniformly confined its attacks to the *male* sex, and among people in the higher and middling classes of society. It has raged chiefly in palaces, castles, halls, and gay mansions, and those things which in general are supposed not to be inimical to health,—such as cleanliness, spaciousness, and splendour, are only so many inducements to the introduction and propagation of the bibliomania!"

It should be remembered, however, that one possessing a fondness for books is not necessarily a bibliomaniac. There is as much difference between the inclinations and taste of a bibliophile and a bibliomaniac as between a slight cold and the advanced stages of consumption. Some one has said that "to call a bibliophile a bibliomaniac is to conduct a lover, languishing for his maiden's smile, to an asylum for the demented, and to shut him up in the ward for the incurables." *Biblio* relates to books, and *mania* is synonymous with madness, insanity, violent derangement, mental aberration, etc. A bibliomaniac, therefore, might properly be called an insane or crazy bibliophile. It is, however, a harmless insanity, and even in its worst stages it injures no one. Rational treatment may cure a bibliomaniac and bring him (or her) back into the congenial folds of bibliophilism, unless, perchance, the victim has passed beyond the curative stages into the vast and dreamy realms of extra-illustrating, or "grangerizing." People usually have a horror of insane persons, and one might well beware of indulging a taste for books, if there were any reasonable probability that this would lead to mental derangement. There could be furniture-maniacs, rug-maniacs, and china-maniacs just as well as book-maniacs, but people do not generally hesitate to purchase furniture, rugs, and china for fear of going crazy on the subject, and no more reason is there why rational persons should hesitate to make a collection of good books for a library, for fear of being called bibliomaniacs. In *Sesame and Lilies* Ruskin says: "If a man spends lavishly on his library, you call him mad—a bibliomaniac. But you never call one a horse-maniac, though men ruin themselves every day by their horses, and you do not hear of people ruining themselves by their books."

This is preëminently the age of collectors, and scarcely a week passes without the discovery of some new dementia in this direction. Only a few days ago I read of a new delirium which threatens disaster to the feline progeny; it may be called the *cat-tail mania*, seeing that its victims possess an insatiable desire for amputating and preserving the caudal appendages of all the neighborhood cats. A self-confessed member of this cult was recently arrested in one of the eastern States.

There are several species of bibliophiles; there are *many* species of bibliomaniacs. Some admire books for what they contain; others for their beautiful type, hand-made paper, artistic illustrations, ample margins, untrimmed edges, etc.; and there are others who attach more importance to the limited number of copies issued than to either the contents or workmanship.

If a book is to attain any considerable commercial value and increase in worth year after year, it is of first importance that the number of copies issued be actually limited; and the greater the restriction the more likelihood that the monetary value will be steadily enhanced. But it must not be forgotten that the mere "limitation" will not of itself create a furore among judicious book-buyers; the book, or set of books, should rest upon some more secure basis of valuation than that of scarcity.

Dibdin says in his *Bibliomania,* issued in 1811: "About twelve years ago I was rash enough to publish a small volume of poems, with my name affixed. They were the productions of my juvenile years; and I need hardly say at this period how ashamed I am of their authorship. The monthly and analytical reviews did me the kindness of just tolerating them, and of warning me not to commit any future trespass upon the premises of Parnassus. I struck off five hundred copies, and was glad to get rid of half of them as wastepaper; the remaining half has been partly destroyed by my own hands, and has partly mouldered away in oblivion amidst the dust of booksellers' shelves. My only consolation is that the volume is *exceedingly rare*!"

The contents, first to be considered, should be worthy of preservation; next in importance is the selection of appropriate type, and the size and style of page, which should be determined by the nature of the work and the period in which it was written. The size of the book and the margins of the page must be carefully considered in order to harmonize with the text-page. In choosing illustrations it is important to determine whether they should be ornate and illustrative, or classic and emblematical in design. The paper should be handmade, to order, and of such correct size as not to lose the deckle edges in cutting; and the printing should be done in "forms" of not more than eight. The paper should be scientifically moistened before printing, and the ink allowed several weeks in which to dry before handling the printed sheets. The bindings should harmonize with interiors, and due care taken against over-decoration of the covers. These few technical hints will serve to acquaint the book-lover with some at least of the many important features which must be regarded in the preparation of a fine book,—a book fitted to demand and merit a place upon the library shelves of discriminating bibliophiles, and as well increase in demand and price whenever thereafter its copies may "turn up" for sale.

Next in importance, after considering literary and mechanical fitness, and the limitation of the work, is the question of distribution; its scope, and the class of subscribers. The stock of a corporation, if limited to a reasonable number of shares and issued only to a few expert investors of high standing, and for tangible considerations, will obviously be considered a safer and more attractive investment than if it be scattered indiscriminately among a class of professional manipulators for stock-jobbing purposes. With such a stock where thus closely held for investment purposes, an order for a few shares may largely elevate its market value. But if the stock were issued in unlimited quantities, the monetary value would be entirely lost. Again, if the stock had no corporeal assets as a basis for its issue, the "limited and registered" clause could not sustain it in the market.

So it is with books: if the number of copies issued be held within a reasonable constraint, consistent with the price charged per copy, and if they are subscribed for by book-lovers who prize them for their literary or historic value and luxurious appearance no less than for pecuniary values, they are not likely to find their way into the bookstalls, or to be "picked up" in auction rooms at less than their original price. This condition applies particularly to legitimate club editions and privately printed editions. If an edition of five hundred copies is widely distributed throughout the country, it is reasonable to assume that the speculative market therefor would be less apt to suffer from congestion than if the sale of the whole number of sets were confined to one locality.

Passing now to those who, in one way or another, are to meet with and handle the completed book, we may begin with a class of *literary barnacles* who stick about the libraries of their friends and of the public institutions, and feed their bibliophilistic appetites on what others have spent much time and money in collecting. These may perhaps more appropriately be called biblio-spongers, and are of all ranks in the community, many even owning beautiful homes, and having ample resources at command; but while enjoying the congenial atmosphere of a well-furnished library, and the delights of caressing the precious and wisely selected tomes of others, they are still of such temperaments that they would no more think of *buying* books than would another of buying an opera-house in order to satisfy theatre-going propensities. These people should be taught that fine books, like friends, are not loanable or exchangeable chattels. They will argue that there is no use spending money for books, because they reside within easy reach of a public library where such books as they desire are readily obtainable, or perhaps suggest that "I have free access to my friend Smith's library; he scarcely ever uses it;" without reflecting that Smith would probably use it more, if his friends used it less. And yet such folk will still incur the needless expense of providing their own homes with chairs, unless, haply, such homes may chance to be within convenient reach of some park or public institution where *free* seats are provided.

Most of us are disposed to idealize a besotted bibliomaniac as a harmless being whose companionship and favor are neither to be courted nor particularly avoided,—a sort of shellfish basking on the bank of life's flow in whatever sunshine it may absorb, and paying little heed to the thoughts or actions of others.

The following curious inscription which is found on an old copperplate print of the famous bibliomaniac, John Murray, will illustrate one of the varieties:—

Hoh Maister John Murray of Sacomb,
The Works of old Time to collect was his pride,
Till Oblivion dreaded his Care:
Regardless of Friends, intestate he dy'd,
So the Rooks and the Crows were his Heir.

Mr. Nathan Haskell Dole, President of The Bibliophile Society, aptly describes a miserly bibliomaniac as a

Victim of a frenzied passion,
He is lean and lank and crusty;
Naught he cares for dress or fashion
And his rusty coat smells musty;

while in characterizing the natural impulses of true bibliophilism, he says that

Bibliophiles take pride in showing
All the gems of their collections;
They are generous in bestowing,
They have genuine affections.

Peignot says a bibliomaniac is one who has "a passion for possessing books; not so much to be instructed by them as to gratify the eye by looking on them."

This presumption is about as reasonable as it would be to say that a man is a monomaniac because he gets married when he is in no special need of a house-servant, or body-guard.

In his *Bibliomania* Dibdin enumerates eight symptoms of this "darling passion or insanity," in the following order: "A passion for large-paper copies, uncut copies, extra-illustrated copies, unique copies, copies printed on vellum, first editions, true editions, and black-letter copies."

The first of these should be omitted from the symptomatic category: it would be fallacy to assume that one is a maniac because one admires the ample margins and paramount qualities of these large-paper copies, which Dibdin himself says are "printed upon paper of a larger dimension and superior quality than the ordinary copies. The presswork and ink are always proportionately better in these copies, and the price of them is enhanced according to their beauty and rarity. . . . That a volume so published has a more pleasing aspect cannot be denied." He adds that "this symptom of the bibliomania is at the present day both general and violent." No wonder! And yet the charming Dr. Ferriar dips his pen in gall and writes the following satirical lines upon this highly commendable "weakness:"—

But devious oft, from every classic Muse,
The keen collector, meaner paths will choose.
And first the margin's breadth his soul employs,
Pure, snowy, broad, the type of nobler joys.
In vain might Homer roll the tide of song,
Or Horace smile, or Tully charm the throng,
If, crost by Pallas' ire, the trenchant blade
Or too oblique or near the edge invade,
The Bibliomane exclaims with haggard eye,
"No margin!"—turns in haste, and scorns to buy.

Dibdin ventures to further assert that "the day is not far distant when *females* will begin to have as high a relish for large-paper copies of every work as their male rivals." If he could return to this sphere and behold the enormously increased number of women bibliophiles in our country at the present time, the subject would doubtless furnish him with a congenial theme for another of his rambling discourses, this time perhaps under the caption of *Bibliowomania*. He was far in advance of the age in which he lived; for although he had very little upon which to base the prediction, he yet prophesied that not many years would lapse before women would invade the fields of book-collecting and prove themselves valiant competitors in the market. This, in fact, is now common enough, and I myself have known of many instances in auction-rooms where a small army of rampant bibliomaniacs have been obliged to retreat and to abandon their pursuit of some coveted treasure, on finding it boldly covered by a *carte-blanche* order from a feminine competitor. Women rarely appear in the book auction-room, but leave their orders to be executed through a trusted broker, and many a collector has found himself suddenly obliged to soar aloft to dizzy heights in quest of some prize, on being thus lifted and pursued by one of the representatives of an unseen and unknown member of the gentler sex.

Many people suppose the term "uncut," characteristic of Dibdin's second "symptom," to signify that the leaves of such volume as may be concerned have never been severed, whether for convenience of reading or otherwise. "Uncut," however, in its technical sense does not imply that the sheets are folded and bound just as they came from the press. The leaves may all be cut, and the tops trimmed, and even gilded, without striking terror to the heart of the bibliomaniac. Dibdin, indeed, treats this last mentioned symptom in merely a superficial way and dismisses it with a few cursory remarks, viz: "It may be defined a passion to possess books of which the edges have never been sheared by the binder's tools." This definition is vague and unsatisfactory. Mr. Adrian H. Joline (*Diversions of a Book-lover*, Harper & Bros., New York, 1903,—a charming book that should be read by every book-fancier) discourses upon the subject more intelligently; he observes that the word *uncut* appears to be a stumbling-block to the unwary, and says: "The casual purchaser is sometimes deceived by it, for he thinks that it means that the leaves have not been severed by the paper-knife. I have read with much glee divers indignant letters in the very interesting 'Saturday Review' of one of our best New York journals, in which the barbarian writers have denounced the *uncut*, and have assailed in vigorous but misguided phrases those who prefer to have their books in that condition. Henry Stevens tells us that even such a famous collector as James Lenox, founder of the splendid library into whose magnificent mysteries so few of us dare to penetrate, was misled by the word *uncut*, and chided Stevens for buying an *uncut* book whose pages were all open. He says: 'Again when his tastes had grown into the mysteries of *uncut* leaves, he returned a very rare, early New England tract, expensively bound, because it did not answer the description of *uncut* in the invoice, for the leaves had manifestly been cut open and read.' When it was explained to him that in England the term *uncut* signified only that the edges were not *trimmed*, he shelved the rarity with the remark that he 'learned something every day.' . . . Perhaps the Caxton Club of Chicago is wise in describing its productions as 'with edges untrimmed.' Even a Philistine ought to be able to comprehend that description, although I once knew a man who supposed that a book 'bound in boards' had sides composed of planking."

Dr. Ferriar's satirical lines in his *Second Maxim* will find sympathizers among admirers of uncuts:—

> Who, with fantastic pruning-hook,
> Dresses the borders of his book,
> Merely to ornament its look—
> Amongst philosophers a fop is:
> What if, perchance, he thence discover
> Facilities in turning over,
> The virtuoso is a lover
> Of coyer charms in "uncut copies."

I have been requested to "explain the reason, if there be any, for leaving leaf-edges fastened [unopened]—even in evanescent magazines—and why people keep books in this condition, without looking at the contents." The reason why the binder does not open all the leaves is that it involves additional labor and expense which the publisher usually does not care to incur, as it does not essentially add to the selling value. Indeed, some collectors hesitate to open the leaves of their books with the paper-knife, for fear that the selling price would be thereby depreciated. This is an entirely mistaken idea, though it prevails very generally among those who do not understand the real meaning of the term "uncut." Most booksellers prefer having the leaves of the volumes all opened, as many buyers and readers object to the nuisance of cutting them open. Some of the magazine publishers have modern folding machines equipped with blades for severing all the leaves. In fine book-making, however, most of the folding and cutting is done by hand.

The third "symptom" defined by Dibdin, viz: "extra-illustrating," commonly called *grangerizing*, is really so far removed from the indicative stages of bibliomania as to render it entirely inappropriate as a proper single characteristic; it is the whole disease in its worst form. Fortunately, it is not a frequent infirmity among our present day bibliomaniacs. I cannot refrain from quoting Mr. William P. Cutter's vehement denunciation of the class of literary foragers who are thus affected. He observes that "this craze for 'extra-illustrating' seizes remorselessly the previously harmless bibliophile, and leads him to become a wicked despoiler and mutilator of books. The extra-illustrator is nearly always the person responsible for the decrepit condition of many of the books which 'unfortunately lack the rare portrait,' or have, 'as usual,' some valuable plate or map lacking. Were this professional despoiler, or his minions, the ruthless booksellers, to destroy the sad wrecks which result from their piratical depredations, all would be well. But they set these poor maimed hulks adrift again, to seek salvage from some deluded collector, or some impoverished or ignorant librarian.

"It is curious that the very volume in which our reverend friend Dibdin so heartily condemns these inexcusable bandits, should be seized on as a receptacle for their ill-gotten prizes. May the spectre of Thomas Frognall Dibdin haunt the souls of these impious rascals, and torture them with never-ceasing visions of unobtainable and rare portraits, non-existent autographs, and elusive engravings in general! They even dare to profane your sacred work, the *Biblia* of book-lovers, by the 'insertion' of crudities invented by their fiendish imagination. They have committed the 'unpardonable sin' of bibliophilism. Not only do they carry on this wicked work, but actually flaunt their base crimes in the face of their innocent brethren. Hearken to this:—

"DIBDIN, T.F. *Bibliomania.* London, 1811. Extended to five volumes, with extra printed titles, and having eight hundred engravings inserted, comprising views, old titles(!), vignettes, and six hundred and seventy-five portraits of authors, actors, poets, sovereigns, artists, prelates, &c., &c., 250 guineas."

Limited space prevents me from making any remarks upon the other five "symptoms," none of which are of any special interest, except to collectors to whose eccentricities they particularly relate.

As to "Autograph Editions," the craze for these continues without abatement. To me, this has always been one of the unsolved mysteries of the book-mania. I can readily appreciate how a collector would prize an author's inscribed copy of some choice edition, but why intelligent people should be allured into the belief that an author's stereotyped autograph displayed upon a front page gives any added value to a set of subscription books, will to me, I fear, forever remain a disentangled enigma. I was once applied to by an agent representing a $6000 "Autograph Edition" of Jean Jacques Rousseau. Having never seen Rousseau's autograph, I asked that it be shown me. "Oh," said the agent, "Rousseau himself don't sign the copies, but the set will be signed by the publishers." Would not a much less expensive and more expeditious way of obtaining publishers' autographs be found in writing a postal card of inquiry for the "prices and terms" on their publications?

Gilpin has left the following quaint account of the eccentric old bibliomaniac, Henry Hastings, the uncompanionable neighbor of Anthony Cooper, Earl of Shaftesbury. The accompanying pen-and-ink sketch represents Louis Maynelle's idealization of this interesting character; it was made especially for this volume:—

"Mr. Hastings was low of stature, but strong and active, of a ruddy complexion, with flaxen hair. His clothes were always of green cloth. His house was of the old fashion; in the midst of a large park, well stocked with deer, rabbits, and fish-ponds. He had a long narrow bowling green in it, and used to play with round sand bowls. Here too he had a banqueting room built, like a stand in a large tree.

"He kept all sorts of hounds that ran buck, fox, hare, otter, and badger; and had hawks of all kinds, both long and short winged. His great hall was commonly strewed with marrow-bones, and full of hawk-perches, hounds, spaniels, and terriers. The upper end of it was hung with fox-skins of this and the last year's killing. Here and there a polecat was intermixed and hunter's poles in great abundance. The parlour was a large room, completely furnished in the same style. On a broad hearth, paved with brick, lay some of the choicest terriers, hounds and spaniels. One or two of the great chairs had litters of cats in them, which were not to be disturbed. Of these, three or four always attended him at dinner, and a little white wand lay by his trencher, to defend it if they were too troublesome. In the windows, which were very large, lay his arrows, cross-bows, and other accoutrements. The corners of the room were filled with his best hunting and hawking poles. His oyster table stood at the lower end of the room, which was in constant use twice a day, all the year round; for he never failed to eat oysters both at dinner and supper, with which the neighbouring town of Pool supplied him.

"At the upper end of the room stood a small table with a double desk, one side of which held a church Bible; the other the *Book of Martyrs*. On different tables in the room lay hawks' hoods, bells, old hats with their crowns thrust in, full of pheasant eggs, tables, dice, cards, and store of tobacco pipes. At one end of this room was a door, which opened into a closet, where stood bottles of strong beer and wine, which never came out but in single glasses, which was the rule of the house, for he never exceeded himself nor permitted others to exceed.

"Answering to this closet was a door into an old chapel, which had been long disused for devotion; but in the pulpit, as the safest place, was always to be found a cold chine of beef, a venison pasty, a gammon of bacon, or a great apple-pye, with thick crust, well baked. His table cost him not much, though it was good to eat at. His sports supplied all but beef and mutton, except on Fridays, when he had the best of fish. He never wanted a London pudding, and he always sang it in with 'My part lies therein-a.' He drank a glass or two of wine at meals; put syrup of gilly-flowers into his sack, and had always a tun glass of small beer standing by him, which he often stirred about with rosemary. He lived to be an hundred, and never lost his eyesight, nor used spectacles. He got on horseback without help, and rode to the death of the stag till he was past four-score."

It is said of George Steevens, the famous Shakespearian collector, that he "lived in a retired and eligibly situated house, just on the rise of Hampstead Heath. It was paled in, and had immediately before it a verdant lawn skirted with a variety of picturesque trees. Here Steevens lived, embosomed in books, shrubs and trees, being either too coy or too unsociable to mingle with his neighbours. His habits were indeed peculiar: not much to be envied or imitated, as they sometimes betrayed the flights of a madman and sometimes the asperities of a cynic. His attachments were warm but fickle both in choice and duration. He would frequently part from one with whom he had lived on terms of close intimacy, without any assignable cause, and his enmities once fixed were immovable. There was indeed a kind of venom in his antipathies, nor would he suffer his ears to be assailed or his heart to relent in favour of those against whom he entertained animosities, however capricious and unfounded. In one pursuit only was he consistent: one object only did he woo with an inflexible attachment; and that object was Dame Drama."

In Dibdin's Bibliomaniacal romance, "Philemon" is credited with the following narrative concerning one who was probably a bibliomaniac in all that the compound sense of the term implies:—

"You all know my worthy friend Ferdinand, a very *helluo librorum*. It was on a warm evening in summer, about an hour after sunset, that Ferdinand made his way towards a small inn or rather village alehouse that stood on a gentle eminence skirted by a luxuriant wood. He entered, oppressed with heat and fatigued, but observed, on walking up to the porch 'smothered with honeysuckles,' as I think Cowper expresses it, that everything around bore the character of neatness and simplicity. The hollyhocks were tall and finely variegated in blossom, the pinks were carefully tied up, and roses of all colours and fragrance stood around in a compacted form like a body-guard forbidding the rude foot of trespasser to intrude. Within, Ferdinand found corresponding simplicity and comfort.

"The 'gude man' of the house was spending the evening with a neighbour, but poached eggs and a rasher of bacon, accompanied with a flagon of sparkling ale, gave our guest no occasion to doubt the hospitality of the house on account of the absence of its master. A little past ten, after reading some dozen pages in a volume of Sir Edgerton Brydges's *Censura Literaria,* which he happened to carry about him, and partaking pretty largely of the aforesaid eggs and ale, Ferdinand called for his candle and retired to repose. His bedroom was small but neat and airy; at one end and almost facing the window there was a pretty large closet with the door open; but Ferdinand was too fatigued to indulge any curiosity about what it might contain.

"He extinguished his candle and sank upon his bed to rest. The heat of the evening seemed to increase. He became restless, and throwing off his quilt and drawing his curtain aside, turned towards the window to inhale the last breeze which yet might be wafted from the neighbouring heath. But no zephyr was stirring. On a sudden a broad white flash of lightning—nothing more than summer heat—made our bibliomaniac lay his head upon his pillow and turn his eyes in an opposite direction. The lightning increased; and one flash more vivid than the rest illuminated the interior of the closet and made manifest an old mahogany bookcase stored with books. Up started Ferdinand and put his phosphoric treasures into action. He lit his match and trimmed his candle and rushed into the closet, no longer mindful of the heavens, which now were in a blaze with the summer heat.

"The book-case was guarded both with glass and brass wires; and the key—nowhere to be found! Hapless man! for to his astonishment he saw *Morte d'Arthur*, printed by Caxton—*Richard Coeur de Lion*, by W. de Worde—*The Widow Edyth*, by Pynson—and, towering above the rest, a large-paper copy of the original edition of *Prince's Worthies of Devon*, while lying transversely at the top reposed John Weever's *Epigrams*!

"'The spirit of Captain Cox is here revived,' exclaimed Ferdinand; while on looking above he saw a curious set of old plays with *Dido, Queen of Carthage*, at the head of them! What should he do? No key! No chance of handling such precious tomes till the morning light with the landlord returned!

"He moved backwards and forwards with a hurried step, prepared his pocketknife to cut out the panes of glass and untwist the brazen wires; but a 'prick of conscience' made him desist from carrying his wicked design into execution. Ferdinand then advanced towards the window, and, throwing it open and listening to the rich notes of a concert of nightingales, forgot the cause of his torments—his situation reminded him of *The Churl and the Bird*—he rushed with renewed madness into the cupboard, then searched for the bell, but finding none, he made all sorts of strange noises. The landlady rose, and, conceiving robbers to have broken into the stranger's room, came and demanded the cause of the disturbance.

"'Madam,' said Ferdinand, 'is there no possibility of inspecting the books in the cupboard? Where is the key?'

"'Alack, sir,' rejoined the landlady, 'what is there that thus disturbs you in the sight of those books? Let me shut the closet-door and take away the key of it, and you will then sleep in peace.'

"'Sleep in peace!' resumed Ferdinand; 'Sleep in wretchedness, you mean! I can have no peace unless you indulge me with the key of the book-case. To whom do such gems belong?'

"'Sir, they are not stolen goods!'

"'Madam, I ask pardon. I did not mean to question their being honest property, but'—

"'Sir, they are not mine or my husband's.'

"'Who, madam, who is the lucky owner?'

"'An elderly gentleman of the name of—sir, I am not at liberty to mention his name, but they belong to an elderly gentleman.'

"'Will he part with them? Where does he live? Can you introduce me to him?'

"The good woman soon answered all Ferdinand's rapid queries, but the result was by no means satisfactory to him.

"He learnt that these uncommonly scarce and precious volumes belonged to an ancient gentleman whose name was studiously concealed, but who was in the habit of coming once or twice a week, during the autumn, to smoke his pipe and lounge over his books, sometimes making extracts from them and sometimes making observations in the margin with a pencil. Whenever a very curious passage occurred, he would take out a small memorandum book and put on a pair of large tortoise-shell spectacles with powerful magnifying glasses in order to insert this passage with particular care and neatness. He usually concluded his evening amusements by sleeping in the very bed in which Ferdinand had been lying.

"Such intelligence only sharpened the curiosity and increased the restlessness of poor Ferdinand. He retired to his bibliomaniacal bed, but not to repose. The morning sunbeams, which irradiated the bookcase with complete effect, shone upon his pallid countenance and thoughtful brow. He rose at five, walked in the meadows till seven, returned and breakfasted, stole upstairs to take a farewell peep at his beloved *Morte d'Arthur*, sighed 'three times and more,' paid his reckoning, apologized for the night's adventure, told the landlady he would shortly come and visit her again and try to pay his respects to the anonymous old gentleman.

"'Meanwhile,' said he, 'I will leave no bookseller's shop in the neighbourhood unvisited till I gain intelligence of his name and character.'

"The landlady eyed him steadily, took a pinch of snuff with a significant air, and returning with a smile of triumph to her kitchen, thanked her stars that she had got rid of such a madman!"

To return, however, to the subject more immediately in hand, it will be observed that the present age is more prolific of bibliophiles than any preceding one, and that the growing interest in collecting fine books is attended by a relatively increasing demand for a higher standard of excellency of manufacture. A few years ago, there were only two or three publishers in this country who "specialized" in fine editions, while at present there are no less than thirty publishing houses, large and small, and as many more "private presses" engaged in the production of beautiful books to appease the demands of book-buyers. Many of these are well established and conducted upon thoroughly honest business principles; some, unfortunately, are not. The publication and sale of books—especially the so-called "de luxe" editions—is, like some other branches of industry, beset with numerous evils; so many sharp practices, indeed, having been resorted to by a few conscienceless publishers, and by a certain class of unscrupulous agents, that buyers have become wary, not to say weary, of being made the victims of their deceptive inventions. It is indeed lamentable that a few such pestiferous schemers should thus bring a certain degree of reproach upon the entire publishing business. It is a common practice among these *soi-disant* publishers—many of whom possess neither capital, credit, nor sense of honor—to buy some lot of etchings or old prints from a junk-shop, or second-hand dealer, at a trifling price, and thereupon work the same off on credulous admirers of rare prints for possibly a thousand times their real value. And it is a common practice for these insidious sharks further to prey upon unsuspecting book-buyers by obtaining publications of reputable houses and falsifying them by the insertion of spurious titles calculated to delude the buyer into the belief that there are "only fifty copies issued." Many of them are ostracized book-salesmen who have at some previous time enjoyed the confidence of their employers, but have been ex-communicated by all honest publishers and booksellers on account of dishonest proclivities. They are therefore set adrift to prey upon the public, and are a constant menace to both publishers and buyers. I shall pay my further respects to these counterfeiters later on when I come to the subject of Book Clubs; in the mean while, it need hardly be pointed out that reprehensible methods of this kind are uniformly condemned among all respectable publishers and book-dealers, and that buyers should cautiously discriminate against those who practice them. It is not surprising that even the honest publishers and dealers themselves are occasionally made the scapegoats of these obnoxious parasites; but the astute collector is rarely "caught" by their schemes; and after a book-buyer has passed the primary or "experience" stages of book-collecting, he (or she) is designated as a "dead one," in the common parlance of the underground trade here referred to. Fortunate, indeed, are the bibliophiles who have passed unscathed into the category of "dead ones."

That my present condemnatory observations are not directed against that great majority of publishers, booksellers, and agents whose methods in business are founded upon sincerity and integrity, will, I take it, be clearly understood; and I am, indeed, forced partially to disagree with Mr. Joline in his vigorous and general proscription of "subscription book-agents," for experience shows that there are many worthy people of this class, however much they may suffer by the sins of some of their kind. An acquaintance once said to me that he would *"never buy another book,"* because he had been "buncoed" by a book-agent, to whom he otherwise referred with an uncomplimentary adjective. But this did not convince me that his position was more logical than that of the man who declared he would never take another bath because a watch had been stolen from his pocket while he was in bathing at some beach resort. It is incomprehensible that any one could imagine that our paper currency system is fraudulent because there are a few "green-goods" men in the country, or because counterfeit bills appear every now and then.

We read so much in the papers nowadays of the extravagant sums paid for rare books by our modern millionaire bibliomaniacs that one is apt to become somewhat panic-stricken upon experiencing the first symptoms of the bibliomania. While these more opulent victims of book-madness vie with one another in the auction-room, the rational bibliophile sits in the gallery and views with silent awe and amazement the scrimmage over some apparently trifling volume that wouldn't fetch ten cents, but for the fact that it is "unique," and that so and so paid a stupendous sum for it at some previous sale. Despair not, dear bibliophile, of never being able to join in the mad scramble for these "uniques;" nor need you feel that they are essential to the formation of a library. They possess no virtues perceptible to the ordinary bibliophile, and it requires all the eloquence of a Cicero to elucidate their charms when displaying them to friends. For after all, the chief point of interest in such books is their cost price, and this you may be obliged to refrain from mentioning for fear you will be accused of being mentally unbalanced.

It is not necessary to squander a fortune in collecting a library, nor to be hasty in buying every book you come across. Better go slowly and select wisely; you will derive more enjoyment from it, and in later years have less to charge to "experience account."

There are a few "busy" book-collectors who intrust the selection of their books to secretaries or librarians, and thus sacrifice the keenest enjoyment of this captivating pursuit. Of all absurdities, this seems the most insupportable. It would be far more sensible to have your secretary select your friends, because if you should happen not to like these, you could abandon them without ceremony or expense. Why not also attend the opera and your various social functions by proxy, through your secretary? If he were as good a courtier as he is "literary adviser," he might succeed in getting as much enjoyment out of the receptions and dinners as you would, if you were to attend in person. Then, think of the *time* you would save! We frequently hear the remark: "I have no time to devote to my library. I am very fond of books, but haven't time to collect or read them." And yet seeing what may be done in this regard by care and system, and that the greatest readers have been the busiest men, it seems strange that persons of intelligence should thus express themselves; should admit such obvious fatuity of view and procedure.

In referring to this class of book-buyers, Roswell Field says, "The book-lover, so-called, who lacks any of the thrills that go with the *establishment* as well as the enjoyment of a library in all of its appointments has deprived himself of many of the most pleasurable literary and semi-literary emotions. That bibliophile never pats his horse or his dog. To him his books are merely tools of trade, accessories to knowledge, to be pawed over, thrown away and replaced by new copies when worn out. He glories in the fact that his books are his servants rather than his companions, and he affects to despise and laugh at the sentimental relation which others have established with their books. Look out for that man! He is not of us; he is not of the elect; there is as little of warmth and the genial glow of fellowship in his library as in the middle gallery of the catacombs in the Appian Way. His very books cry out against him; but he hears them not, for he is deaf as well as blind."

One of the busiest men in New York City, whose name is familiar in financial circles throughout the civilized world, is one of the most voracious collectors of the age. He probably transacts more business in a day than half a dozen ordinarily busy men, and yet finds time to give his personal attention to every minute detail of his vast collections, to which are added hundreds, and probably thousands, of items every year. This is only one of many such examples among our busiest men.

I have often heard persons lament in a pensive and apologetic sort of way, "Yes, I have a great weakness for fine books." The very presence of this mis-called weakness, however, is unmistakable proof of great mental strength, and those who suffer from it may find solace in the fact that the giants of commerce, leading statesmen, and great men of affairs in general are frequently thus afflicted all through the periods of their greatest activity and success. What can possibly afford a more agreeable relaxation from the toils and perplexities of the day than to recline in an easy chair before an open grate fire in the library, surrounded by the silently reposing tomes which record and preserve the noblest thoughts of past and present generations? Surely no enjoyment in the home or office can be more delectable and unfailing in assuaging the worry and solicitude of a strenuous life than the silent companionship of books. It is a noteworthy fact that a large percentage of the leading stock brokers, bankers, active statesmen, and sedulous lawyers are bibliophiles. I attribute this to the fact that all of these vocations are extremely taxing upon the nervous system, and those men who are busily engaged in them are, during the intermittent hours of rest and recreation, naturally inclined to seek the most enjoyable and refreshing diversions; for, as Horace says,—

> . . . nunc veterum libris, nunc somno et inertibus horis
> Ducere sollicitae jocunda oblivia vitae.
>
> Along with old books, or a nap, and divine hours of leisure—
> To taste thus forgetfulness—sweet, in the midst of life's troubles.

In an article written for The Bibliophile Society's (1903) Year Book, Caroline Ticknor says, "The true book-lover loves his books for their helpfulness, for their companionship; but he regards them as well for their elegant settings." She also observes that "strange as the anomaly may seem, there are still many persons of ample means, and some education, who, although they would be horrified at the very thought of admitting to the home a cheap rug or vase, to destroy the harmony and bring discord and confusion into the luxuriance of the furnishings, yet will nonchalantly tolerate the incongruity of a miserable fragment of a library made up of the cheapest and meanest editions to be found in the market, such as would be scorned by those of the most limited means and plebeian tastes. These will be found inappropriately housed amid the most sumptuous surroundings. A single rug to adorn the floor, or a single vase resting on a mantle, will often be found to have cost ten times as much as the whole home library. And yet the intellects of these people have been nurtured and trained in their youth by the brilliant thoughts of ancient and modern writers! Even the favorite author, be it Shakespeare, Dickens, Longfellow, Tennyson, or some other, is frequently represented by a half dozen or so disconsolate-looking volumes, the remainder of the set either never having been bought, or else, if bought, thrown aside, or strewn around the attic, or abandoned as a child would discard a toy which afforded it no further amusement.

"It is worthy of remark, however, that the enormously increased demand of late for beautiful books evinces the fact that cultured and wealthy people are growing to appreciate the importance not only of having a good library, but that its quality should embody a degree of estheticism to correspond with the surroundings."

Many of the most delightful persons, well read and competent to discourse intelligently upon the merits of books and authors, have never experienced a single pulsation of true bibliophilism; they have never known the joy of possessing and admiring a beautiful book, and that the attachment one bears for such a treasure is wholly reciprocal. They have not learned that fine books, like human beings, are capable of mutual affection, and that it is not necessary to devour them in order to value their charms. "We do not gather books to read them, my Bœotian friend," says Mr. Joline; "the idea is a childish delusion. 'In early life,' says Walter Bagehot, 'there is an opinion that the obvious thing to do with a horse is to ride it; with a cake, to eat it; with a sixpence to spend it.' A few boyish persons carry this further, and think that the natural thing to do with a book is to read it. The mere reading of a rare book is a puerility, an idiosyncrasy of adolescence; it is the *ownership* of the book which is the matter of distinction. The collector of coins does not accumulate his treasures for the purpose of ultimately spending them in the marketplace. The lover of postage-stamps, small as his horizon may be, does not hoard his colored bits of paper with the intent to employ them in the mailing of letters. When some one complained to Bedford that a book which he had bound did not shut properly, he exclaimed, 'Why, bless me, sir, you've been *reading* it!'"

Herrick says that "the truest owner of a library is he who has bought each book for the love he bears to it; who is happy and content to say, 'Here are my jewels, my choicest possessions!'" Seneca, the great Roman philologer, wrote: "If you are fond of books, you will escape the *ennui* of life; you will neither sigh for evening, disgusted with the occupations of the day, nor will you live dissatisfied with yourself or unprofitable with others." "I am quite transported and comforted in the midst of my books," says the younger Pliny, who was an ardent book-fancier; "they give a zest to the happiest and assuage the anguish of the bitterest moments of existence. Therefore, whether distracted by the cares or losses of my family or my friends, I fly to my library as the only refuge in distress: here I learn to bear adversity with fortitude."

Southey thus immortalizes his speechless, yet beloved, library companions:

My never failing friends are they,
With whom I converse day by day.

Balfour is no less eloquent in paying worthy tribute to his library: "The world may be kind or hostile; it may seem to us to be hastening on the wings of enlightenment and progress to an imminent millennium, or it may weigh us down with the sense of insoluble difficulty and irremediable wrong; but whatever else it may be, so long as we have good health and a library, it can never be dull."

"Bookes," said the immortal Milton, "demeane themselves as well as men. Books are not absolutely dead things, but doe contain a potencie of life in them to be as active as that soule was whose progeny they are: nay they do preserve as in a violl the purest efficacie and extraction of that living intellect that bred them. Unlesse warinesse be us'd, as good almost kill a Man as kill a good Book; who kills a man kills a reasonable creature, God's Image; but Hee who destroys a good Booke, kills reason itselfe, kills the image of God, as it were in the eye."

In the garnering of book-treasures, some collectors are prompted wholly by mercenary motives—most of them, fortunately, are not. There are biblio-mercenaries of such sordid inclinations that they would readily part with almost any book in their possession,—even inscribed presentation copies!—if lightly tempted with money considerations. Verily, these parsimonious traders would barter their own souls, if they possessed any value.

I am indebted to the Secretary of a well-known book club for the following facts, to confirm which I saw all the correspondence. A certain book-buyer joined the club some time ago, and subscribed for the first publication issued after he became a member. Upon receiving the work he wrote: "I consider them among the most beautiful examples of book-making that I have ever seen, and prize them above all other books in my library." Six months later he sold the copy to a book-agent for twice its original cost. He "passed" the next publication issued by the club, as it did not interest him, but appended a postscript to his letter, saying: "If any member wants an extra copy, I have no objection to one being issued upon my membership and turned over to him, provided I receive the increase in price."

The following humorous incident is recorded in the (1903) Year Book of another prominent book club. It may be explained that the club issued a very elaborate and beautiful publication, printed upon deckle edge handmade paper, illustrated with remarque proof copperplate etchings on Japanese vellum, and in duplicate without remarque on Whatman paper: "One of the members upon receiving the first two volumes of the — — publication, writes: 'The Society starts out by making the worst kind of a blunder. The man's picture in the front of the volume is put in twice and on *two kinds of paper*. I could excuse this error, but imagine my horror when upon turning to the back of the volume I found the *same mistake repeated*. This is too much.' He closed by expressing a desire to resign, saying that he did not know he 'was joining a faddists club,' and takes occasion to remark further that 'the books are cheaply finished, not even being trimmed and gilded;' also that he 'can buy better books in the stores, *with full gilt edges*, for less money.'"

So much has been written about the vagaries of book-collectors and bibliomaniacs that the subject has long since become threadbare, and about the only unexplored field of labor left to the choice of him who would gain a hearing with the reader—if one can be found who is not already weary of reading what the wags think of his (or her) own peculiar whims—is to fall in with the spirit of the age and compile an "International Library of the World's Greatest Gibberish about Bibliomaniacs." We have the "World's Greatest" everything else in book-lore, and I shall not be surprised if some enterprising publisher gets out a "definitive" *de luxe* edition of the "World's Greatest Dictionaries." Indeed, the Holy Bible itself has not escaped, for they are now making a "de luxe" edition, in fourteen volumes! to be sold by subscription. It will not be an "Autograph Edition," however.

The freaks and fancies of capricious book-gatherers and bibliomaniacs have undergone so few changes in the last hundred years that modern writers on Bibliomania, after vainly searching the horizon for some new development in the way of symptoms of the disease, or characteristics of those afflicted, have wandered off into the verdure of adjacent fields to avoid repetition. Some of them, from sheer lack of anything new to say, have set upon each other in the most unflattering terms. Many of the writers on the delectable "Joys of a Book-buyer," or "Habits of a Bibliomaniac," etc., evidently appreciate the fact that these much persecuted human beings have other pastimes and habits than collecting books, and that they really inhabit the earth in all its civilized parts and partake unstintedly of its many pleasurable diversions. But again, there is another extreme, for I once read a book issued under the misleading title of "Pleasures of a Book-collector," or something of the sort, which might have been more appropriately called the "Pleasures of a Single Man," seeing that the work had more to do with the hero's hopeless love for a fair damsel, and his hours at clubs, cafés, and other places of amusement in which I had no special interest, than it did with the acquirement of literature. Thus, with the delusive idea that I was to be ushered into some of the secret enjoyments of the pleasing diversion of book-buying, I presently found myself more familiar with the habits, vices, and various unimportant matters of the author's conception—points, in short, having no bearing whatever upon the subject under consideration—than with the pleasures of a book-collector. The book was not badly written, nor wholly uninteresting; but if a man buys a ticket to the opera, he doesn't go prepared to see a cock-fight.

For literary scoffers and malcontents who find fault with everything and everybody, who even scold publishers because their own books bring but meagre royalties, who fuss and fume over the harmless foibles of the very ones upon whom they depend for their audience, and like an ungrateful dog fasten their teeth in the charitable hand that offers them food, there can be but small sympathy. One is tempted to enlarge upon this familiar type, but here I am digressing from my subject, and am committing much the same offence as that of which I have elsewhere accused others.

I have been asked to include within the scope of my article a few remarks about Book Clubs and Book Societies. In presuming to trespass upon sacred yet inviting ground of this character, I must be understood as approaching the subject with due reverence and apology. It is an indisputable fact that among the agencies that have contributed to the advancement and ennobling of the bookmaker's art in the past twenty years, the legitimate Book Club has been one of the most potential. We have only to refer to *Growell's American Book Clubs* in order to learn of the many clubs and societies of this kind which have arisen in the past few years, with varying degrees of success and failure,—success, when intelligently conducted upon honest coöperative principles, and failure, if irrationally directed, without regard to the maxims upon which successful clubs are managed. The province of these worthy accessories in the world of fine bookmaking has not been free from invasion by sharks and charlatans, some of whom have succeeded for a time under the guise of honest and reciprocal motives.

In this country there are private book clubs and societies that have won places of enviable distinction both here and abroad, and naturally among the foremost of these are the ones which have been pestered by "imitators." The following significant remarks are taken from the president's annual address to the members of an old and honored book club:—

"Fame brings its penalties, and during the last year many of us have suffered considerable annoyance, both individually and as members of the Club, through the exploitation of books advertised sometimes as publications of The —— Club, and more often as publications of the —— Society. These have usually been offered in connection with works of distinguished authors in numerous volumes, stated, as a rule, to be limited to a thousand copies, and described as the contents of the private library of a lady, which the agent declares to have been placed in his hands to dispose of as quickly as possible, regardless of cost. No widow's cruse, apparently, could be more unfailing in its supply than this 'private library.' While annoying, the device of a '—— Society,' though manifestly designed to confuse the public mind and trade on the reputation of this Club, can scarcely deceive our members or even the book-loving public. It, nevertheless, is an annoyance, and the more vexatious because scarcely calling for other remedy than exposure.

"It is possible, however, that harm to the good name of the Club may be wrought through the advertisement, in an English newspaper, to which my attention has been drawn, of a so-called '—— Society of Great Britain,' which is declared to have been recently formed in conjunction with the '—— Society of the United States,' which is described as having been established in 1884, and to have occupied its own Club House since 1888, and to have published handsomely printed books for sale exclusively to the members. It is announced, however, that the '—— Society of Great Britain,' although intending to act in conjunction with the American society, 'will work upon somewhat different lines, at any rate at first.' It may well be that this cleverly deceptive advertisement will require some attention from us, either directly or through members resident abroad.

"This, however, seems to be the only fly in our ointment, and we may congratulate ourselves that there is nothing more serious to disturb our enjoyment of the anniversary which we now celebrate."

Another and more palpable fraud has been perpetrated in copying the name of The Bibliophile Society, but with a slight prefix, just enough to afford a loop-hole through which to escape legal prosecution. Not enough, however, to enable the public to distinguish between the spurious and the genuine, and even the members themselves have sometimes been deceived by unscrupulous agents representing their wares as the regular productions of the valid society. The audacious promoters of this so-called Society had the boldness not only to pilfer the name of the legitimate society, but also the name of its president, which was ostentatiously printed upon their letter heads, together with the name of Dr. Richard Garnett. Both of these gentlemen have recently published their denunciations through the columns of the press, and protested vigorously against this unauthorized use of their names.

The *modus operandi* of this pestiferous concern is to send numbered "complimentary certificates" throughout the country to persons whose names are obtainable from directories, and when acknowledgment cards are received from those who deign to accept the exalted compliment, they are forthwith called upon, usually by some "officer" of the Society,—sometimes the "President," but usually the "Treasurer," "Secretary," or "Registrar."

Some time ago I was honored by a call from one of these circumventive "Treasurers," but happened to be conveniently busy at the time, and so made an appointment with him to meet me at my office the next day. Meanwhile, I prepared to have his statements reduced to writing by a stenographer, anticipating that it might be necessary to refresh my memory upon certain passages that I might fail to remember verbatim. The following is the substance of the "canvass" as taken by the stenographer in an adjoining room, the door of which was wide open:—

"I am the Treasurer of the —— Society, with headquarters in London. By a special grant from the English Government, we have recently been permitted to extend our membership into this country, and three hundred life members are to be admitted under this enlargement of our constitutional privileges. It may interest you, first, to know something of the origin of this Society. It was organized in London about three hundred years ago by the Duke of Roxburghe [who was not born until more than a hundred years later], and was originally composed of about thirty members of the royal family. The original charter limited the membership to fifty members, and in less than a month the limit was reached. Through the powerful influence of the royal family the Society had easy access to all the great repositories of unpublished manuscripts, and the most valuable and interesting of them were selected for publication. These publications became so enormously valuable that it stimulated a desire on the part of others to join the Society, and particularly, some of the nobility of France and Germany. It was decided to increase the membership to three hundred, and to take in a few members from France, Germany, Italy, and Russia. The Society thrived for about a thousand years [this is either a stenographic error, or else he meant to say a hundred]; then there was a period of inactivity, and later on it was revived again, and the membership limit increased to five hundred. Last year we obtained permission to again increase the membership by taking in three hundred prominent people in America. I am over here to arrange for three vice-presidents,—two for the East and one for the West. I have a special commission to ask you to become one of the honorary vice-presidents and to offer you a life membership for less than half the regular fee, viz., $225.00; the usual fee for life membership is $500.00, but you get it for $225.00 on account of acting as our honorary vice-president for this territory. Of course you would have no regular duties to perform. You would sign all the membership certificates in your district, and in case of the death of any member, you would have the privilege of naming his successor.

"The Society issues every year a volume giving all the price currents for the year, and keeps the members posted on the advance or decline in the value of all important publications. We also give you in confidence the ratings of various publishers, and print reports to members exposing all the frauds in the book business. Upon payment of the fee of $225.00, you receive all of this material free, for the balance of your life, and in addition all of the Society's regular publications, including the present one, consisting of —— volumes [here he produced the customary specimen sheets]. You see this one work alone is worth the full amount you pay for life membership [here occurred a "special offer" of some sort, given in a low monotone which the stenographer was unable to hear; and I must confess that I was so stupefied by this astounding fabrication that I myself have not the faintest recollection of what this "special offer" consisted]. We are very anxious to have your name as our honorary vice-president here, because you will not only be an honor to the Society, but the Society will be an honor to you."

Here my Treasurer friend produced a regular form of subscription contract for a set of books; but it contained no clause about life membership, or any other membership, and included no promise of anything further than the delivery of the books.

The honor of such a vice-presidency being thrust upon me was indeed a thrilling sensation, and the story was told in a fluent, cohesive, and logical manner; so well, in fact, that had I not known in advance that it was purely imaginary from beginning to end, I could scarcely have avoided giving it full acceptance. But I had heard of the story before, and although partially prepared, it staggered me surprisingly. I afterwards learned that every one else canvassed by my interviewer was equally offered one of the "three vice-presidencies."

There appears to be no defense for book clubs against these bogus impersonations. The injured club, or society, can sustain no claim for any special damage, because, as not offering its publications in the open market, it actually suffers no ascertainable loss of patronage. The principal damage results to those who are thus victimized in permitting themselves to be deluded into the belief that they are acquiring the valid editions of reputable clubs. When club publications come into the open market they are usually picked up with avidity by collectors, and they have thus grown into very general favor among book-lovers. Indeed, the high esteem in which they have come to be regarded offers a productive field for a few crafty publishers to ply their wily designs in. The audacity of these schemers carries them to such incredible measures that they sometimes buy sheet-stock from reputable publishing houses, change the name of the edition, and deliberately manufacture new titles on which they print the name of some book club or society. These counterfeits are sold to the unsuspecting book-buyer, who often imagines he has landed a prize. Later, he is likely to become disillusioned. There can be no doubt that the contemptible practice of thus mutilating and garbling books should be defined as a felony and made punishable by fine or imprisonment. Book-buyers, however, can in a measure help the situation and protect themselves by not dealing with such people; they should particularly remember that creditable book clubs *never* employ soliciting agents, and rarely, if ever, offer their publications for sale outside of the membership. Any one, therefore, representing himself as an authorized agent of a book club may usually be branded as an impostor. Most book clubs print only such number of copies of each publication as are subscribed and paid for by members in advance, and the funds thus advanced are used to pay the cost of the edition.

Notwithstanding the evils referred to, the book club is with us to stay, and the very fact that it is continually pestered by these hangers-on is conclusive proof of its potency and usefulness; features which insure its secure foundation in the community.

Very few people are able to appreciate the amount of gratuitous labor performed by the officers and committees of private book clubs. It is erroneous to suppose that beautiful books are a purely natural offspring of the book club. The preparation of the material for publication and successfully following it through all the various stages of manufacture requires an enormous amount of detail work, as well as an accurate knowledge of bookmaking. The president of a prominent book club recently said, in his annual address to the members:—

"I wish that our members could be witnesses at the many conferences held by the Committee on Publications and by the Council; of the various experiments needed to settle upon the size and shape of the book, the size of its page and its margins, the style of type, the initial letters, head-bands, tail-pieces, engravings, etc. etc.; of the printer's endless proofs, the making of a special paper (which sometimes proves to be unsuited), and, finally, the style of binding. What material, color, and general make-up shall it have? If our members could thus follow the progress of the work from beginning to finish they would be reconciled to disappointment. At any rate it is through their subscriptions that these experiments can be undertaken, and it is by knowledge thus gained that the Club has won credit for the Arts and Crafts of our country, and made an honorable record even in other lands; so that to be a member of the Club has become an enviable distinction."

Owing to the tricks and stratagem practiced in *manufacturing* "de luxe" editions, some of our bibliophiles have taken matters of bookmaking into their own hands, with the result that they have organized clubs and societies, the members of which take much pleasure in introducing to their library companions each year one or two charming new acquaintances which come bearing the club's seal of endorsement. A true bibliophile always feels a just pride in shelving one of these book-treasures of his own club's production, and thereafter displaying it before his friends, with the interesting bit of information that "This is the latest production of *our Club*; it is issued *only for members*." For obviously an owner's interest in any work is increased many fold by the fact that he is a constituent part of the organization which produced the same: the relationship to the book in such a case is akin to the love of a parent for a child; and the owner of a fine library will not unusually regard his Club publications and privately printed books as the objects therein which are entitled to his fondest consideration.

I have recently taken occasion to examine with considerable care the latest publications of the leading book clubs of this country, and to compare them with some of the first issues of these same clubs. The improvement in the later productions over the earlier ones astonished me. There were as good artists, editors, binders, type, paper, ink, and other accessories twenty years ago as we have now, and indeed it is doubtful if our modern printing presses show much improvement in the quality of work during that time; but it would seem that persistent effort along the lines of experimental work has been generously rewarded by a steady improvement in the general results now attained. Nor is the situation injured by a slight tinge of friendly rivalry among clubs, to lend an additional zest to their labors, and to whet the praiseworthy ambition of each to make every succeeding issue a little better than the last. There are many zealous bibliophiles who belong to two or three book clubs at once, finding it interesting to collect and compare the works produced by the several clubs.

Many of our great scholars as well as leading publishers are members of these book clubs, and serve on the councils and various committees; so it must not be supposed by skeptics that their publications are in the slightest degree amateurish. They employ the best talent and materials; the councils and publication committees, as well, being composed of persons of unquestioned integrity, who possess an intelligent understanding of bookmaking.

Some of these clubs (particularly those whose membership is largely local) have commodious quarters where the members may meet at all times, whether to discuss matters of common business interest, to exchange their latest jokes, or to generally discuss book-lore and other congenial topics. The social features of some of the book clubs are, however, reduced to the occasions of the annual meetings and dinners. The "Club-Room Question," in one of these organizations having a membership of five hundred, distributed in one hundred and sixty-seven cities and towns in this country and abroad, was recently reported upon by the Council as follows:—

> The question of providing and maintaining club rooms and establishing a suitable library for the Society has been more or less discussed since its incorporation. The Council has not found that spacious and luxuriously furnished rooms are an important requisite in accomplishing the expressed purpose and limitations of the Society. These, according to Article I. of the Constitution and By-laws, are to be "the study and promotion of the arts pertaining to fine bookmaking and illustrating, and the occasional publication of specially designed and illustrated books, for distribution among its members at a minimum cost of production."
>
> Then, too, while our membership is entirely homogeneous in bibliomaniacal spirit, it is so scattered over such a vast expanse of territory that only a small percentage of the members would be able to enjoy club-room privileges; even those within easy reach of such rooms would probably not frequent them enough to justify any considerable expense in maintenance. It would be necessary, also, to change the present constitution (and to assess the members for annual dues in order to meet current expenses), should the club-room idea be carried out. This would be objectionable on various grounds, and amongst these, because a non-resident member might thus be paying an annual fee without receiving any corresponding benefit in return; a condition in such case which would be tantamount to his meeting an increased charge each year for the privilege of subscribing and paying for the Society's publications. Hence, the Council do not see their way to entertaining or recommending the club-room feature. But it is not supposed that the spirit of fellowship among our bibliophiles—naturally related as they are by a kindred interest—will in any degree suffer because of the lack of such facilities. A personal contact, however agreeable, does not seem essential. Certainly the many charming letters received from members whom we have never seen, go far to relieve the present lack in this regard, so far as the officers are concerned.
>
> As matters now stand, the Society has sufficiently comfortable quarters in one of the offices of the Treasurer, where the Council holds its meetings. These are found by experience to be quite ample for all practical purposes and present needs.

Collectors of manuscripts and of unique copies often furnish the book clubs with valuable and otherwise unprocurable material to be printed for the members. Last year one collector alone furnished gratuitously to a society of which he is a member, many thousands of dollars' worth of unpublished manuscripts of interesting historical matter to be printed exclusively for its members. In this way much valuable material is preserved in print, when it would otherwise remain forever unpublished and unobtainable.

During the past few years it has been my pleasant privilege to spend many hours of each week in concurrent labor with the Council in the preparation of the publications of The Bibliophile Society, in which Council I have had the honor to serve continuously since its organization.

There is no pleasure more delectable, no joy more inspiring than that of devising books which prove a delight to the eye and a satisfaction to the artistic tastes of those who are competent to appreciate the qualities that should characterize a perfectly made book.

I now realize as never before why it is that our busiest men of affairs, and scholars of renown, are actuated to serve so assiduously in this labor of love; for surely no amount of effort, however laborious, can be regarded as having been in any sense misguided or wasted when it elicits such approbation as expressed in the following letter from Charles A. Decker, Esq., a fellow member, of New York City:—

March 15th, 1904.

Mr. H. H. Harper, Treasurer,

The Bibliophile Society,
Colonial Building, Boston, Mass.

Dear Mr. Harper:—

My stock of superlatives is insufficient to adequately express my appreciation of "André's Journal." Keats must have had a psychic sense which enabled him to see the latest issue by our Society, and he had this in view when he wrote the opening line of *Endymion*. (Is n't "A thing of beauty," &c., the opening line?) Such books as the Council has planned are an education to bibliophiles; the work is progressive, for each issue is finer than the one which preceded it. Can any book be finer than "André's Journal"? If so, I can't conceive it. Such noble types, the pages so perfectly balanced; the margins so broad; the paper of such beautiful texture; the ink so brilliantly black; the maps so marvelously reproduced; the etchings so artistically conceived and executed and the title page so beautifully engraved; then the binding—real vellum—so rich, simple, and in such perfect taste; even the box-cover is fitting in every sense. A perfect book, it seems to me. If there are any shortcomings, and you know them, don't tell me of them, that in my ignorance I may be content.

Please thank all the members of the Council for me. Somebody must have spent many, many hours in arriving at a final judgment upon all the parts which make up such a beautiful whole.

I have yet to enjoy the pleasure of *reading* the "Journal," then I will be thankful to Mr. Bixby and to Senator Lodge.

Yours sincerely,
(Signed) Charles A. Decker.

Mr. Decker is one of the many pleasant and appreciative members of The Bibliophile Society whose personal acquaintance it has not been my good fortune to make, but from whom the Society has received many delightful and inspiring letters. The numerous communications thus received from all quarters have been placed before the Council, with the result that the individual interest of every worker has been greatly augmented in the Society's welfare. Indeed, I attribute no small measure of the success and the good name of the Society to the indirect influence of such words of encouragement and expressions of appreciation as have come from the members.

I sincerely wish for health and continued success to our worthy Book Clubs, and regret that there are not more of them.

Sit bona librorum . . . copia.

Henry H. Harper.

Lector House believes that a society develops through a two-fold approach of continuous learning and adaptation, which is derived from the study of classic literary works spread across the historic timeline of literature records. Therefore, we aim at reviving, repairing and redeveloping all those inaccessible or damaged but historically as well as culturally important literature across subjects so that the future generations may have an opportunity to study and learn from past works to embark upon a journey of creating a better future.

This book is a result of an effort made by Lector House towards making a contribution to the preservation and repair of original ancient works which might hold historical significance to the approach of continuous learning across subjects.

HAPPY READING & LEARNING!

LECTOR HOUSE LLP
E-MAIL: lectorpublishing@gmail.com

Printed by Libri Plureos GmbH in Hamburg,
Germany